I WANT TO BE A SUPERHERO

WRITTEN & ILLUSTRATED BY
MICHELE GMITROWSKI

Copyright © 2020 Michele Gmitrowski.

Cover and Interior design by Michele Gmitrowski

This is a short story children's book.

All rights reserved.
No part of this book may be reproduced or used in any manner without written permission of the copyright owner except for the use of quotations in a book review.

This book is dedicated to
All first responders who have proven to be our
Superheroes and who are there for us day in
and day out

I want to be a Superhero

Just like on TV

But Superhero's aren't always

Like that...

They can be like you and me

Just continue reading and believe me

You will see

They grow up and learn special things

That will help the world...

Just you wait and you will see

All the things that they have Learned

A doctor is a superhero

And I know you will ask why...

He can fix you when you are sick

And he does not need to fly

A fireman helps people

And in a big red truck he comes

He saves so many people

And stops fires when they burn

A teacher shows us how to

Read and write and spell...

We can learn so very much

Because she teaches us so well

A policeman is there to help us
when we feel afraid...

If something bad happens he helps to
make us brave.

He will help you and will guide you if ever
you are alone...

All your parents have to do is dial for him
on the phone

A farmer is a person who grows our food...

Like, potatoes and carrots

To Make a stew

He has cows, pigs and chickens too

I mean without him what would we do?

A nurse is there to help you

To guide you for your needs

She knows just how to care for you

And knows just how you feel...

She'll keep you safe and check you before you see a doctor

And if you don't feel well

She will take your temperature

A construction worker builds for us
Our homes, our schools, and more

He works outside in the rain

And even in the snow...

He builds our roads and bridges

So we can travel here and there

And this also helps us, to go just anywhere

The dentist is there to help us

When a tooth hurts way too much...

They fix your pain with a filling

And do it with a gentle touch

A veterinarian is awesome

Especially when my dog is sick

She knows just how to treat him

For that he gives her a lick...

That's his way of saying thank you

Without our veterinarian what would we do?

Now a pilot is like a superhero

Because he knows how to fly...

He flies in a big airplane

That goes really, really high

When we go on vacation and it is pretty far

A pilot gets us there safely

When we cannot get there by a car

So you see that a superhero can be many things

There is no need for a cape, special powers Or wings

As you grow up you will see a superhero can be just like you and me...

As you grow and get older in school you will learn...

With hard work, you'll get a good job in return

About the Author

Michele Gmitrowski was born in Calcutta, India, but raised in the United Kingdom from the age of four. When she was sixteen, she and her family immigrated to Canada, where she still lives today. Her heritage is a mixture of Spanish, Irish, Armenian, and British. As a child, Ms. Gmitrowski was a tomboy-always playing soldiers with the neighborhood kids, and loving to write detective stories as a pastime. As she grew older, she became a lover of poems, and eventually had one of her own published in 2004, in VoicesNet Anthology. She also had a book published in 2019, The Darkness Within by Inkwater Press, her memoir, And a Mystery Thriller, Seduced By a Predator by Inkwater Press/Ingramsparks in 2020. She has always wanted to write a children's book, and did her first two in 2020, also.

Michele Gmitrowski was born in Calcutta, India, but raised in the United Kingdom from the age of four. When she was sixteen, she and her family immigrated to Canada, where she still lives today. Her heritage is a mixture of Spanish, Irish, Armenian, and British. As a child, Ms. Gmitrowski was a tomboy-always playing soldiers with the neighborhood kids, and loving to write detective stories as a pastime. As she grew older, she became a lover of poems, and eventually had one of her own published in 2004, in VoicesNet Anthology. She also had a book published in 2019, The Darkness Within by Inkwater Press, her memoir And a Mystery Thriller, Seduced By a Predator by Inkwater Press/Ingramsparks in 2020. Ms Gmitrowski is happily married and has two wonderful children (a son and a daughter), as well as four grandchildren. Her family makes her feel quite blessed.

www.ingramcontent.com/pod-product-compliance
Lightning Source LLC
Chambersburg PA
CBHW051305110526
44589CB00025B/2940